Free Trade:

How To Get What You Want Without Spending *Any* Cash!

Frank J Dobrucki

FREE TRADE:

How To Get What You Want
Without Spending Any Cash!

ISBN: 978-0-692-81812-1

Library of Congress Cataloging-in-Publication

Printed in the United States of America

Crestview Press books are available for business, education, and promotional discounts. For information, please contact marketing at: publisher@crestview.press or by mail: 3571 E. Sunset Road #102, Las Vegas, NV 89120

CRESTVIEW PRESS

Table of Contents

Dedication

*T*his book is dedicated to my friend and colleague Saul Yarmak.

In the early '80s, Saul was a major shareholder in the original "BX," which later became "BXI." After a lengthy legal battle, he was able to gain control of the company and took it private. During his time running BXI, Saul oversaw tremendous growth and expansion. He was generous with the trade brokers and earned an enduring reputation. In the mid '90s, Saul was approached by two investors who claimed to want to invest in his company and help him grow his business. This is what he really wanted. After completing the first round of investment, it became clear that the two investors were straw buyers for a rival competitor who had made several offers and had been refused. Another legal battle ensued and only after a judge advised Saul that because the other company was publicly traded, a lot of investors would be harmed if he did not agree to settle the lawsuit, did he finally agree to sell the balance of the company. Many years later, Saul told me that he had not been ready to leave the barter industry when he agreed to sell the company.

"Let's see how things turn out this time around!"

Introduction

When is a great idea still a great idea? How about when it can pass the test of time? New ideas come and go, and most have only a small window of time in which they can truly be relevant. But great ideas will continue to thrive, even surviving under difficult circumstances. If you don't kill it, imagine the potential that can occur when you finally get it right!

In 1960, a Southern California banker named Mac McConnell created a new company called BX (Business Exchange). His great idea was to develop a modern barter company that would operate much like a bank with offices across the country and tens of thousands of business owners trading goods and services — without having to spend cash.

BX was set up as a franchisor, selling territories across the country. The problem with selling territories is that most will never be developed, and once someone has already tied up an area, it creates an obstacle in recruiting talented people who could otherwise develop a strong business. All these layers of people, from the corporate office to the franchisor and local offices, need to make money. The main source of revenue needs to come from the membership base.

As you can imagine, any company set up by a banker will have a variety of fees. The BX fee structure included a $495 membership fee to join the organization, followed by fees of $12 in both cash and trade each month and a 10 percent cash fee that would be assessed on each and every trade transaction. Credit lines were offered to members at 1½ percent per month (18 percent annually). Bankers love their fees!

Many people will tell you that BX took off like a rocket and created the modern barter age. But did it really? Tens of thousands of businesses joined BX — and an industry did grow. Still, fifty-plus years later, the entire barter industry has only a small number of independent exchanges, with no company having more than 20,000 **active** trading members. Less than 200,000 **active** trading members belong to barter exchanges in the entire country. In my opinion, this industry should have at least 10 million members in the U.S. alone.

What barriers have limited the number of businesses willing to participate in a practice that will result in growing a business and saving money?

I believe that while McConnell had a great idea, his financial model was seriously flawed. Many exchanges have come and gone, and the entire barter industry continues to struggle without any clear giants in the industry. I also believe that if we "fix" the flaw, we will finally see the modern barter age come to life and truly explode.

Consider that around the same time the original BX was being introduced, another financial innovation was being launched by the banking industry. BankAmeriCard, which later became known as Visa, was introduced to 60,000 customers in Fresno, California. This was the first bank credit card to launch into an unknown market. After a bumpy start and after soon discovering a new criminal enterprise in credit card fraud, the industry finally took off. Today, Visa alone has more than 1.4 billion cardholders.

One very unique feature of Visa is that the company does not lend any money. Visa provides an infrastructure base, which is licensed to thousands of banks and financial institutions, which then lend money to their customers through the Visa platform.

The original BX also introduced a unique financial platform that can be replicated and licensed to financial institutions to provide yet another layer of service to their customers.

The potential of an explosive new industry utilizing a strong global trade currency is still waiting to happen.

Chapter 1

A Brief History

As I mentioned in the introduction, BX was the first company to be credited with creating the modern barter age. The company operated for more than 40 years, during which time the company name was changed to BXI and was sold several times. In 2005 a competitor acquired BXI; the membership was assimilated into the new parent company and BXI ceased to exist.

In the past 50-plus years, many companies have come and gone. What is clearly amazing is that all of these companies are utilizing a similar financial model that McConnell introduced with the original BX. The only real changes are higher fees and the idea of splitting the trade fee to charge 50 percent on the sale side and 50 percent on the buy side of each transaction.

In 2001 two very large startups raised over a hundred million dollars and both were set to completely revolutionize the barter industry. Big Vine, a company with the backing of American Express, set out to tap into millions of cardholders and merchants. I can't believe that nobody saw the potential conflict of marketing a business where "money-is-an-object" to a group of cardholders who believe that "money-is-no-object." After opening up elegant corporate offices and hiring lots of executives, Big Vine failed.

The next big hitter up to bat was Intagio. What was so unique about Intagio is that they actually acquired BXI as part of their startup. Even with the name of the most respected company in the industry, Intagio was unable to explode the barter industry into a household brand.

So what went wrong? Why did both of these well-funded operations fail? First, you have to realize that until these two operations started, barter was a small community business. Local brokers signed up local businesses and kept the trade deals close to the community. Most brokers feared the impact of outside members and tried to protect their members. Big Vine and Intagio had the right idea, but the wrong strategy. The barter industry should be able to be replicated and grown not only as a national model, but a global model. The biggest problem was that both relied on the basic fee structure that McConnell introduced in 1960. Big Vine eliminated and reduced fees the most, but fees are still fees in the eyes of the consumer.

This time around the focus will be on establishing a "Global Trade Currency" that can adapt to all aspects of trade instead of the traditional trade exchange or barter club. Once a strong standard trade currency is established, many new opportunities will become available and the size of the trading community will grow to numbers that have never been imagined.

Chapter 2

What is Trade?

Trade involves the transfer of the ownership of goods or services from one person or entity to another in exchange for other goods or services or for money. Possible synonyms for "trade" include "commerce" and "financial transaction." A network that allows trade is called a market. [Wikipedia https://en.wikipedia.org/wiki/]

The original form of trade or barter saw the direct exchange of goods and services for other goods and services. Barter is trading things without the use of money. Later one side of the barter started to involve precious metals, which gained symbolic as well as practical importance. Modern traders generally negotiate through a medium of exchange, such as money. As a result, buying can be separated from selling or earning. The invention of money (and later credit, paper money and non-physical money) greatly simplified and promoted trade. Transactions between two traders is called bilateral trade, while transactions between more than two traders is called multilateral trade.]

Before there was money, everything was purchased and sold with trade. So how do we properly define trade? It's not money, and it's not even anything tangible. Trade is basically the original form of an IOU. Unless both parties are walking away from the table with merchandise, trade is a promise to pay based on a certain value expectation for what is initially received.

Today there are many forms of non-cash value systems. Many are called alternative currencies, crypto-currencies, and shadow currencies. Trade would be known as an alternative currency, which is defined as any form of lending or financial record keeping that does not go through the banking system. Most of these currencies can also be described as digital currencies simply because most do not print any monetary bills or stamp metal coins. Thus, the only way to store, record, earn, and spend is through electronic methods.

Most alternative currencies are contained by demographics or a particular industry. In 2006, BerkShares, a local currency that circulates in the Berkshires in Massachusetts, was launched with the purpose of supporting approximately 400 local businesses. BerkShares actually prints its own money and then sells the currency at a small discount on the dollar to encourage local residents to patronize the local merchants. To date, over 7 million BerkShares have been issued from participating local banks.

In 2009, Bitcoin was launched and created a global frenzy with the idea of a true Internet based crypto-currency. There was a lot of buzz about the anonymity of the inventor and the idea of absolute independence from banks and government authority. Bitcoin has proven that it has real value and that it is a viable form of electronic currency. In 2015, more than 100,000 merchants were willing to accept payment with Bitcoin.

Here's my issue with Bitcoin. As this is a currency that is easily convertible to a cash currency, what advantage is there in marketing to a client base? To me, the ideology of Bitcoin is really no different than making the choice of payment — i.e. which credit card, debit card, or checking account — I will use to buy something. Where is the financial advantage that separates the economics of the transaction?

The main advantage is that you do not have to convert from one international currency to another and you are

17

operating under the radar. The main purpose of crypto-currency is to be able to move money on a global basis without having the financial oversight of the banking industry. The huge disadvantage is that because Bitcoin is set up as a peer-to-peer system, the Bitcoin currency is actually stored on your computer. If your computer crashes, then your Bitcoin currency is virtually wiped out and you cannot restore it — ever! This one point alone is enough for me. Most Bitcoin wallets arrange to convert your Bitcoin into your local currency as soon as possible.

This is probably the biggest difference in alternative currencies. If a currency is convertible to cash, you are most likely going to convert it. We like the feeling of having lots of cash. The idea of stuffing your mattress with cash is tied to the idea that nobody can steal your precious money when you are sleeping on top of it! We like having cash in our wallets, in bank accounts, and stashed in safe places.

Trade is the only alternative currency that acts a counterpoint to cash. Trade is not convertible to cash. You can sell trade at a discount, because nobody is going to pay you equal to cash. If you consider BerkShares, these local dollars are sold at a small discount to give the people buying and using them a reason to consider purchasing them — because they are going to save an extra 10 percent when they support local merchants.

Unlike most alternative currencies, trade is the one currency that you can spend when you do not have the money to make a purchase with cash or a cash-convertible currency. Trade brings an entirely new economic engine to the table. The advantage of trade is that you are clearly going to save a significant amount of real money when you participate in trade transactions. All members in a trade deal are going to maximize the value of their products or services by realizing only the actual cost involved. The one feature that separates trade from the majority of alternative currencies is how easy it is to earn. Most of the cash-convertible currencies are going to have the same issues of attracting buyers because parting with an equal to cash product is just like spending your cash. Trade is not convertible, so it sits outside your pile of cash or cash-convertibles. Trade is much easier to earn. The savings to buyers are substantial so they are going to see if they can acquire something with trade before spending any cash or cash-convertible currencies first. For larger merchants, specifically companies that want to reduce inventories or clear out merchandise before introducing a new product, trade is king! Instead of having to write down the value, trade brings in the highest price. In many instances, much larger transactions can be completed in one swing and then resold to the members of a trade exchange later. This makes trade easy and convenient because many companies can decide how much trade they want to generate and complete the transaction in a relatively short period of time.

The annual volume in the alternative currency industry in just the trade & barter sectors will exceed $20 billion dollars per year. When you consider this is an industry that has never truly matured into the powerhouse platform it should be, the opportunity for enormous economic growth is an inevitable certainty.

The final questions in properly analyzing trade should be: Is trade too small for your business? Or is your business too small to trade? Realistically any business can trade. It's just a matter of making the decision to participate in another economic platform that can greatly impact the profitability of your existing business.

The crazy part about trade is that everybody is already doing it in one form or another. Think about how many times you have offered to do something for someone without using money. Most people don't even realize they are trading. The big challenge now is to harness the concept and start using it on a regular basis to truly make a difference in your economic life.

Chapter 3

Why Trade?

While many people might be looking for a compelling reason to participate in the barter and trade market, my question is, "Why *not* trade?" Trade is such a common sense product. This is a financial tool that has real value and is extremely easy to generate. It does not replace money, but operates alongside established monetary currencies.

As I talk to people, I tend to get the same question: "Is this like Bitcoin?" The answer is, "No, trade is not like Bitcoin." Bitcoin is a crypto-currency that operates the same way money does. Bitcoin is fully convertible to cash currencies. The huge appeal to Bitcoin is the anonymity that you can move cash without having to go through banks. You can buy and sell Bitcoin for cash. Trade is a totally separate currency that is not convertible to cash.

Perhaps I can use a couple of examples of how trade can help with existing situations. Consider a bank that has loans on commercial real estate. Whenever property values decline, the banks auditors will review the value of the secured assets versus the existing loan balances to determine whether the bank has sufficient cash reserves on hand to cover losses in the event of a default. This is a nightmare for a bank because it basically has to put money aside to protect its interest in these loans. When the banks auditors recommend increasing the amount of loss reserves, this becomes an escalating burden. Many banks prefer to get rid of the toxic paper on their books, even if the loans are current, and many times offer a 10 to 30 percent discount as an incentive to pay off the loan early and remove it from the books. On a million dollar note, this could be a three hundred thousand dollar discount.

According to bank math, it is easier to write off the loss once the loan is off the books, because it will no longer require any cash reserves. This is a situation where I think trade could dramatically improve the situation. If the bank were to offer the note payee the same cash discount, with the balance (30 percent) to be paid in trade, the bank would not be showing a loss of any kind on this loan. I am not changing the original deal of offering the discount, but by adding the trade component there are several unseen advantages. For the bank, there is no compromise to accept trade instead of cash. The bank was already willing to take a loss by discounting the note.

Let's look at this from the customer's side of the equation. If the bank discounts the note, it may issue a 1099 to the IRS to reflect the discount, turning the discount into untaxed revenue. This could be extremely expensive for the customer. Next, the discount could also affect the valuation of the building because you cannot continue to depreciate an asset at a higher value than what you paid. You would have to adjust the value downward, which could reduce the tax benefits.

A recent hotel sale in Las Vegas saw a bank agree to a selling price more than two billion dollars less than the principal amount of the loan. This was an enormous loss. The bank could have recovered at least one billion of the loss through trade. The hotel would have repaid the trade over a period of years with empty rooms. The result of paying a higher price with a combination of cash and trade would have given the new hotel owners a higher basis price, which would have contributed to more tax deductions. The trade portion would not have cost anything to carry as debt.

The inclusion of trade in financial transactions can also attract a lot of new buyers. The two examples I have used both saw the banks accepting much less than they could have realized without the benefit of trade.

I am definitely not advocating that anyone pay a higher price to gain tax advantages. That would be ridiculous. What I am suggesting is that trade is an excellent vehicle to stabilize values in a declining market. The real estate industry does not have any concept of value stabilization. We all watch the market get hot and prices climb higher and higher, and then, just as it always happens with every cycle, the bubble bursts and then we all watch prices go lower and lower. In the end, a lot of people end up losing a lot of money and a small group of investors pick up assets at fire-sale prices. We need to use a stabilizer to moderate the value and slow down the meltdown effect. Trade is the only product I have ever encountered that can accomplish this task.

Most people still do not understand that trade is a valuable commodity and is also a valid financial instrument that can greatly assist in transactions. It is time to figure it out! We are talking about millions and billions of dollars here. I have only touched on the sale side of the transactions. Let's look at the much bigger picture.

Trade is a recognized currency. The Internal Revenue Service recognizes trade as "equal to the U.S. dollar" for taxation purposes. This means that any company can list the amount of trade either in a bona fide trade account or as an obligation on its financial statement. Trade is an asset. Trade contracts can easily be sold and converted into trade currency.

A lot of media companies, newspapers, magazines, radio, and television companies do a lot of trade deals. Many times this means a file cabinet of scrip (gift certificates) or IOU documents. I met with executives at a television station who were bragging about the great trade they had with airlines. Unfortunately, when they showed me a stack of airline tickets, they realized eight of the ten tickets they were counting on using had already expired.

A magazine executive complained about how employees hovered around whenever a trade deal was closing to see if they could get some of the benefits as either a perk or a bonus. Trade is revenue! If you treat trade as something less valuable, it will slip through your fingers.

The smart thing to do with trade is to sell whatever you are not going to use in the immediate future through a retail trade exchange. You are now converting your trade into a currency and recording the transaction as revenue.

You can build up a balance of trade and then direct this account for things that you would normally spend cash to purchase. Once you have arrived at a place where you are able to generate a steady flow of trade and then use it as a substitute for cash purchases, you are efficiently managing trade and more importantly, saving cash every time you pay with trade instead of cash. What other financial instrument gives you this much flexibility?

There are many reasons why you would want to trade. First of all, it's fun! Trade is a lot easier to generate than cash and there are many things you can do with trade. The most important reason to trade has to be the ability to reach your financial goals.

I remember the first transaction I did with a trade exchange. I was closing an office and had a very large, heavy, and expensive executive desk and credenza that I no longer needed. It was a high-quality product and I did not want to put it into storage to sit somewhere for years and years. A local trade broker brought one of his wealthier clients to see the desk. The guy looked it over and said: "I'll give you $3,000 trade for the desk." I responded that my price was $5,000 and it was the only price I would accept. He responded that it wasn't worth $5,000, at which point I gave him the name and address of an office furniture store located a few miles away.

They had the same desk set on sale for $6,000 cash. About 30 minutes later, he returned and happily agreed to pay me $5,000 trade for the desk. The transaction was easy and resulted in a much higher price than I could have gotten had I tried to sell used furniture in a cash market, and the best part was that now I did not have to move it. That sucker was heavy!

It's interesting that today the online marketplace for selling used stuff is exploding. The main difference with cash and trade is that cash will always bring a lower price than trade. As cash is valued higher, people are less willing to part with it and will negotiate much harder to get a deal. Trade is earned at cost, which is usually between 25 to 30 cents on the dollar. This means that while you may pay significantly more, your actual cost is still lower than the price you could have negotiated with cash.

Starting a home business can cost a lot of money. Are you properly organized and do you have the right setup that properly reflects the professionalism you are trying to portray? Do you need a professional website? Do you want to advertise to expand your reach? These are all things that can get very expensive and that you can easily pay with trade.

For artists, there is no better option than trade. Artists need to establish value by selling their art. A sale for trade is equally valid. The trade revenue can be used to print fliers, invitations to exhibits and installations, and cover travel expenses. Art and jewelry are two categories that do not move very fast, but the markups more than make up the difference. There is really no business that cannot benefit from the expansion into the trade market. The best way to increase the value of trade is to grow the number of businesses that accept trade transactions. The larger the overall membership base grows, the larger the opportunities for trade expands.

If you have a positive trade balance and want to do business with a company that is not a member of the trade system, give them a call and tell them that you would really like to do business with them. As you are already a member of the trade system, all they need to do is join, and then they will have a guaranteed customer.

Chapter 4

Modern Trade

The modern barter industry was created in 1960, with the first effort to monetize trade as a currency. One of the problems of trade is getting both sides of a transaction to arrive at the same valuation. Most independent trades are lopsided with one party contributing more than the other party. Many times the, "I'll catch you later" idea of completing the imbalance of the trade transaction never happens and people feel like they were taken advantage of. The idea of introducing a "trade-currency" into the mix solves this problem. Instead of trading either an item or service for another, each party sells to the other for an established price or value. It doesn't matter what the other party has to sell, because the trade currency keeps each trade level and completes each transaction. You don't even need two parties to trade with each other any longer. As long as buyers have already traded before and accumulated trade currency in their accounts, they can spend their trade with anyone who is willing to accept trade.

It's kind of funny that the "modern barter industry dates back to 1960." There were no computers or Internet. Stamps and checks were used to post transactions. It took time to deposit checks and clear the transactions. In many cases, only a few transactions could be completed each month with the same trade dollars. Today, with smartphone apps and websites, transactions can be completed electronically, making it possible to complete several transactions per day with the same trade dollars. The speed and efficiency of trade contributes to being able to take advantage of great opportunities.

People are motivated by the deals they can put together today and not over a long period of time. If a seller is motivated to purchase something, he will be much more motivated to sell whatever product or service he has at an aggressive price to raise the necessary trade dollars needed to complete the transaction. Speed is an important component in making good deals come together.

Trade is a virtually limitless component. There is no industry that cannot be stimulated or expanded with the inclusion of trade. But many hurdles need to be cleared for trade to be more universally accepted. The first hurdle is the size of the membership. The larger the membership base grows, the larger the trade opportunities will be available to the entire membership. The second hurdle requires the most discipline. Many people view trade as a temporary transaction where you can liquidate items you acquire with trade to cash at a steep discount. This ideology truly devalues the overall potential of trade as a viable economic alternative to cash. The solution to this problem is to establish solid relationships with sellers of coveted goods and services, which will be purchased to "keep" instead of sold off at a discount for cash. The more valuable trade transactions become, the more solid the platform becomes as a truly viable economic stabilizer.

There is no reason why large purchase transactions cannot be financed. Securable assets, which are financed with cash, can also be financed in a similar way with a trade currency. I believe this practice will allow trade to be more widely accepted and respected as a currency alternative.

If you consider the real estate industry, many people believe that market forces drive real estate prices. How many times have you seen real estate prices drop dramatically and many people lose huge amounts of equity? When real estate prices start to recover, greed moves in and then prices start to climb at alarming rates, with people rushing to try to buy something before the prices get too high. What comes next is always the same thing, the market softens and then another dramatic drop in price. The real estate market is a classic example of the "blind leading the blind." Real estate prices are always compared to current sales. Appraisers use current sales to value a property by what a buyer is willing to pay for a particular property. Lenders depend on the appraised value of a property to determine whether they will agree to extend a loan. When real estate prices drop, all the appraisals on property become virtually worthless. They are no longer a valid measure of value. What the real estate market needs is a way to stabilize the price component of property. This is one area that I truly believe trade can become an amazing component.

Why should a bank or lender be willing to accept trade for real estate? Trade is always earned at cost, so there is always a generous spread. For the sake of argument, let's say that the cost component in this exercise is 50 percent. If a lender is foreclosing on a commercial building, in a soft market, the lender will have to sell the building at a significant discount to attract a buyer. Selling the building for less than the previously established value will cause the lender to experience a loss, but the greater problem is that the valuation of all the neighboring properties will also be affected. This is a true domino effect. The idea of accepting a trade transaction at the full established value would certainly shore up the value of the neighboring properties and now you are not waiting for "market-forces" to wait until the market hits bottom.

Let's say we are talking about a million dollar building. With the "market-forces" approach, the lender would probably be able to get $600,000 for the property. Once you consider a real estate commission and the holding costs, the lender will probably only realize $500,000 — experiencing a 50 percent loss on this particular property.

Next let's consider a trade transaction where the buyer is willing to pay the full value of one million dollars for the building. As we mentioned before, the trade buyer has a 50 percent cost in his trade currency, so the buyer is willing to pay a higher price than the softened market price. Here is where it gets to be fun! The buyer will be able to book the new asset at one million dollars, with full proof of purchase. This is a valuable addition to a financial statement and the tax benefits will be based on the full purchase value. The lender will not show a loss on the transaction, which will help in the overall stability of the lending institution. As larger trade transactions are completed, the faith in the value of the trade currency will also grow, meaning that adding trade currency holdings to the financial statement of a lending institution will also help to stabilize financial markets.

If you consider a person who donates a building to a non-profit organization rather than see the value plummet, this is not always an easy transaction. The non-profit organization has to hold the building for a long time to maintain the write-off for the donor. Non-profit companies are not usually in the business of managing buildings. Just the fact that the building is being donated should signal a weakening of the economy. In a weakened economy, buildings will face more vacancies, resulting in higher costs to manage and market the building. If the non-profit sells the building for less than the donation price, the donor will lose part of their deduction.

Now let's look at the process another way. If the donor first sells the building for trade, at the full value price, and then donates the trade currency to the non-profit, there is no chance that a future sale of the building will have any effect on the donor's deduction.

For companies that want or need to sell off large inventories, cash is usually king; however, by utilizing a trade transaction instead, the company could still show a profit on the transaction. The real issue at hand is whether or not the company can utilize the large amount of trade that inventory reductions can create. Each company needs to evaluate its cash expenditures to see where some expenses can be substituted with trade, thereby conserving cash. If a company can utilize trade to pay for expenses instead of cash, the company comes out a winner. The first thing you need to do is write down a list of the items that you normally pay for in cash. The next thing is to determine which items can be purchased with trade. Every dollar you substitute with trade saves you money.

Chapter 5

Who Can Trade

The reality is that everybody already trades. All businesses participate in some form of trade. It's second nature to want to trade. There are many different names for trade; barter or trade are two words that are interchangeable. Due bills, countertrade, ledger accounts, in-kind donations, store credit are all forms of trade that eliminate cash from transactions.

So here is a good question: "If everybody is already trading, why do we need another trade system or exchange?" What we need is one that really works. None of the current operations have ever grown to a size that can even make a dent in the amount of trade that is already occurring around the world. What we need is a common trade currency that can be used throughout all levels of trade, along with a common platform where members can trade with each other. With so many forms of electronic communication, from smart phones, tablets, computers, etc., it only makes sense that members will be able to communicate and trade more efficiently with each other.

A common "global trade currency" can then be used as the base for multiple exchanges, including international organizations and community currency groups. The real benefit is that all of the trade members would be participating in strengthening a single platform. Multiple organizations increase the opportunities to trade and offer many more members, all with goods and services to contribute. The larger the overall membership base grows, the more solid the trading currency becomes. There is no way that a small independent exchange with a few hundred members could ever compete with a well-balanced trade organization with hundreds of thousands or millions of members. If you are going to trade, why not seek out the strongest and most reliable trading environment?

Once you have made the decision to trade, the next step is to make sure you can get the things that really matter with your trade currency. If you cannot find a particular item you want, the best way to get this item is to call the provider directly. Let's say you want a painter to paint some offices. Tell the painter you belong to a trade organization and that you are interested in giving him your business. Refer him as a new member. If he chooses to join, he already has business waiting for him. If he chooses not to join, then tell him thanks anyway, but you will look for another painter until you find one who is willing to accept trade currency. Most people do not want to walk away from a sure thing.

Trade is really a community event. While a lot of transactions can take place anywhere, most trade takes place locally. Just like the local businesses you patronize on a daily or weekly basis, trade relationships work exactly the same way. Once people realize that the value of their trade transactions is solid and that the currency is strong, repeat business is a sure thing. When businesses start to turn down new trade business because they have too many credits in their account and feel they can't get what they want when they want to trade, the system starts to slow down.

Each business member of a trade group has the right to determine how much trade he wants to accept. If a member tells you he is at his limit, this is not always a bad thing. The business member may actually have accepted a lot of trade and needs to pace himself so that he can spend what he has earned before accepting more. If the member is telling you that he needs some cash in the deal or tries to steer you away from trade, you are being played. The solution to members trading fairly is two-fold. First, there needs to be enough variety of members in each category so that members have a choice of whom they want to do business with and second, each member needs to be vigilant about how he spends his trade. If you believe your trade has value, then spend it like you spend your cash. There are people in the marketplace who will gladly overcharge you — if you let them. If you are willing to say no to a cash deal that doesn't make sense, then use the same internal guidance when negotiating with trade.

It is the trade organization's job to ensure that the trade currency you are using has real value and is properly managed and accounted for. It is your job as a member to spend your trade wisely. If you are cautious and feel that you are getting valuable goods and services with your trade currency, then you will be satisfied and open to accepting future trade transactions.

Trade is such a common sense practice. It should make total sense to everybody, yet you will always have people who need constant training or encouragement to understand that what they are doing is a good thing and that they will benefit from participation.

Investment companies are always trying to convince people to invest with them, even though many clearly lose money that their clients invest. Trade is not an investment. Trade is another form of currency that lives in a place alongside cash. Trade is an economic vehicle that can help you achieve your financial goals. The final outcome is determined by how well you manage the trade you have earned and what you have to show for the trade you have spent, just like you would with the cash you have spent.

The reality is that anybody can trade, just like anybody can be successful and rich — if that is what they really want. It doesn't usually happen by accident.

Chapter 6

The Value of Trade

Every commodity has a "cost" value of what it actually costs to purchase or earn the final credit. In the trade industry, there are many different platforms for trade. The barter industry is generally a retail trade platform. In retail trade, members of a trade exchange sell goods and services at standard retail prices to other members of the exchange. The actual cost of goods is the basis for the trade credits and the spread is the percentage of profit realized in the transaction.

A good example of retail trade is a restaurant. Prior to accepting trade customers, a restaurant is already in business. The costs of running the business, rent, utilities, and salaries of employees are already being covered by the cash business coming in. When a new business agrees to accept trade, the purpose is to bring in additional revenue. You realistically can't expect to allocate all of the business expenses into each trade transaction. If the restaurant has empty tables, there are no additional costs of rent, utilities, or employees to serve a few additional meals. The only cost you can realistically attribute is the actual food cost. The industry average for food costs is approximately $0.28 on the dollar. This means that the cost of earning a trade dollar for this particular restaurant is 28 cents. The flip side means that every time a trade dollar is spent, instead of a cash dollar, the savings will be 72 percent.

If this same restaurant now spends an average of $1,000 per month in trade to purchase advertising, which attracts new cash customers, the actual cost of the monthly advertising is $280, saving the restaurant $720 per month.

On an annual basis, the restaurant would need to earn $12,000 in trade income to cover the advertising contract. The actual costs to the restaurant would be $3,360 and the savings would be $8,640. The restaurant will see revenue increase by $12,000 solely because of the trade transactions and the increased advertising should bring in additional cash revenue, without the need to recover the advertising investment like most businesses do.

Every business hits a revenue plateau. This is quite normal and you have to understand what promotional products you need to utilize to gain a larger market share. Many times, a business is lucky just to break even on the costs of an advertising promotion. Why spend money when it is not going to bring you additional revenue and profits? Well, that's what everybody does! Advertising is an extremely necessary component of a successful business. Many times, a business needs to invest a substantial amount of money into advertising to establish their brand and gain consumer awareness.

The main difference with trade is that it does not require spending any advertising money to attract. Customer acquisition costs are a normal expense in attracting cash customers. The economics of trade include a built-in stimulus component. Because trade transactions can save such a large percentage, there is an economic driver in place to move transactions forward. The ability to generate trade revenue is primarily based on a desire to participate in the market.

Let's face it — cash will always be king! If you are rolling in cash, you probably don't need to trade. If you can use the extra revenue that can be earned through trade, all you need to do is "want to trade." Not all businesses are equal and some are going to attract trade much easier than others. The trade marketplace is filled with buyers who are all earning trade at cost and are ready to save when they spend their trade instead of cash.

As a trade buyer, you have to be vigilant in your purchasing habits. There are lots of crooks in the cash world; just imagine how much easier it is to overcharge or take advantage of trade customers, because they are saving money with each transaction. If you feel that someone is asking too much for a product or service because the price is in trade, bring it up to the owner or manager of the business. If you don't feel right about the transaction — don't buy it! Even sellers willing to trade have to compete for business.

Many people in business try to "bait and switch" to attract new customers and then change the deal. Trade really works well when sellers are willing to accept 100 percent trade for a deal. It generates good feelings between the parties and more and more people are willing to trade with fair prices. Some businesses will say they have a high cost of materials and that they need to get some cash in the deal. Amazingly, these same people want to be able to purchase with 100 percent trade when they are on the buying side. I have considered the possibilities of different levels of trade membership, with the 100 percent group at the top and the 50/50 percent group who are only able to purchase at the same terms. This gets very complicated and I think unnecessary. We are all grown ups. If a buyer thinks a deal is fair — then make the deal. If more buyers hold out for 100 percent deals and the businesses that are asking for cash can't get any business, then they will have to change their business model to participate.

The most important thing for each and every trade member to realize is that the trade credits you have earned are yours to spend. If you are careful and plan beforehand to substitute purchases that you would normally pay for in cash, you are going to save money and keep more of your hard-earned cash. Once you have considered your business expenses, the opportunities for spending trade are endless. As a trade exchange community evolves, there are always new members and new opportunities available to the membership.

A curious thing about trade transactions is that most buyers think the exchange is involved in every transaction. This is not true. The exchange is a third-party: the record keeper of the trade credits that books the transactions between the parties. The transactions always occur between a buyer and a seller. If either party is dissatisfied with the outcome of a transaction, then the parties need to come together to solve their disputes. You would not call your bank and tell them that someone did not perform as expected. There are federal laws regarding credit card transactions, but they are very limited. In trade transactions, the exchange is not a party to the deal. Members have the same legal rights as cash customers. If an offending party is not living up to its side of the deal, the courts and/or consumer rights programs are available to settle disputes. It is important for a trade exchange to know which members are mistreating members so that they can be monitored and/or canceled if necessary.

The more vigilant trade members are in getting good deals, the stronger a trade currency will become. A good rule of thumb is: "If you wouldn't make the same purchase with cash — don't do the deal with trade."

You can protect yourself by not paying for anything until you have received what you are purchasing. Just because you are not spending cash does not mean that you have to be any less vigilant about your trade resources.

One of the nice things about trade is that you have to be a member of a trade exchange to be able to participate. In the cash world, you deal with total strangers on a daily basis. There is a sense of community in the trade world, which makes for better relationships and better awareness of the products and services that are available to trade.

Trade also has the advantage of being able to employ brokers when needed. If you are trying to complete a large project, either in selling a lot of products or services, or looking to buy a lot of products or services on trade, you may find the services of a certified trade broker to be beneficial in sourcing the right trade partners to make it happen. With modern technology, members can list their products and services in marketplaces and directories for free so that other members can find trading partners. There is so much flexibility available to all members.

Ultimately, the real value of trade is determined by how much you want to participate.

Chapter 7

The Old Deal

When the modern barter age was developing in the '60s and '70s, the program was mostly presented by salesmen who pitched the benefits of trade. The membership fee to join a trade exchange was usually in the $495 to $695 range. Potential members were told about how many things they could buy with trade and that they would receive lots of new customers for which they only had to pay a 10 percent commission. Who wouldn't be willing to pay a paltry 10 percent commission to get new business? A 90/10 split does not seem like a bad deal, and in reality it is not a bad deal, even when you consider that the new business will be paid in trade and that the commission would be paid in cash.

When you look at the economics of trade, this is a very viable concept that can save a business from spending a lot of its cash and have the ability to leverage its extra capacity or excess inventory. One of the disadvantages of the old deal was that there was no equality of membership. Members who traded the most also paid the most fees. It makes sense that the members who pay the most also get the most attention and get first crack at the best merchandise that is available. This made for a very imbalanced system.

The membership was divided into areas with brokers who felt they had to protect the trade within their own systems. It wasn't until 25 years later that the idea of splitting fees was put into practice so that brokers would be willing to work with members from outside their area. Prior to that, there was no incentive to accept business from members who were not a part of your area. The whole idea of areas was also a really bad idea. If you have three or four independent brokers in one major city, and each broker signs up 500 members, you now have a trading pool of 2,000 local businesses to trade with. The idea of one single broker being able to handle that much business, let alone be up to the challenge of reaching that many people, is crazy. It never happened. What you ended up with was areas having far fewer members than they could have had if they had opened the areas up to more competition. It's not like multiple brokers could have signed the same member. There was no competition problem. Once a member is signed, he cannot be signed again.

When you look at the largest trade exchanges, usually only 10 to 20 percent of the offices are making enough money to maintain a staff and make a decent living. That means 80 to 90 percent of the members cannot be properly serviced. There was always a huge imbalance in the overall structure, yet everybody paid the same percentage of fees.

I am not trying to focus only on the problems. As I stated earlier; "Great ideas will continue to thrive, even surviving under erroneous circumstances. If you can't kill it, imagine the potential that can occur when you finally get it right!"

My belief is that if you take a really good look at the positive and negative attributes of the trade exchange world and get rid of the negatives, the possibilities are waiting to be discovered.

The whole idea of paying so many fees actually acted as a deterrent for optimum growth and stability of a trade exchange system. What you want is a system that will only keep growing and enhancing the opportunities of all the members without reaching a ceiling and stalling out.

Chapter 8

Hidden Benefits

The most important realization about a trade currency is that it is an asset. Trade currency is a financial commodity, just like everything else listed on a financial statement. The fact that it isn't cash shouldn't make you think it is worthless. Stocks and bonds are not cash either — until you sell them. If you are in a hurry to sell, many times you will experience a loss. You have to understand the difference and then maximize the opportunities of each unique benefit.

The U.S. barter industry is compliant with TEFRA (The Tax Equity and Fiscal Responsibility Act of 1982) based IRS 1099B reporting requirements. This means that every year all members of barter organizations will receive a 1099B for all of the trade dollars/credits earned for the previous year. The IRS considers a trade dollar to be equal to a U.S. dollar for tax purposes.

This one fact causes a lot of people to be concerned because this means that trade income is also taxable income. Here is a very important thing to understand. When something is "taxable," it is also "deductible." If you are using your trade revenue to make purchases that you would otherwise be making with cash, you are saving cash on all of these purchases. If the purchases you would have been making with cash are deductible, then the same purchases using trade dollars will also be deductible. There is no difference in the treatment of either cash or trade for taxation purposes. This is such an important benefit because many people do not realize that you can take advantage of the deductions of trade transactions.

Trade is treated the same way cash is treated when reporting gains. If you are selling a product in trade, then you obviously have a cost basis. If you are running a business, then you are probably already scheduling the "costs of goods" for your inventory. If you have not deducted these costs, then you will need to do this in order to get the true gain from sales on trade.

Disclaimer: Please do not take anything written in this book as accounting or tax compliance advice. Please consult a tax professional for your own financial reporting matters.

Another very important benefit is the accounting of cash equivalents on a financial statement. The balance of trade credits in your account should be listed on a financial statement, along with cash, investments, stocks, bonds, etc. You need to understand that trade currency is another financial asset that needs to be identified with all other financial assets.

Probably the most important benefit of trade is income enhancement. Your business is worth what it makes. Many people think that if they show less income, they will save money on taxes. Not a great idea! Aside from being an illegal practice, it also lowers the value of your business. Anybody who owns a business wants to increase revenue on a continual basis. This is how you grow your business and how your business increases in value.

One of the best examples of the real benefit of trade is a hotel. If you consider a 200-room hotel with an average 80 percent occupancy, this means that on average, 40 rooms will be empty each night. An empty room generates zero revenue. Accepting trade brings in a full night's rate for each room occupied with trade customers. In addition, all hotels have auxiliary revenue streams like restaurants, bars, shops, soda and snack machines. Trade customers also spend cash. Many businesses make additional revenue. Determining which level makes sense to offer in trade will create the opportunity for additional revenue to be generated as well.

Most hotels and restaurants rely heavily on word-of-mouth recommendations from satisfied customers. It makes no sense that trade customers would only tell other trade customers about their experiences. To the contrary, I believe the majority of people who hear about an excellent meal or wonderful stay at a hotel would be non-trade customers, only enhancing the future cash business opportunities for the business.

The value of a business is directly determined by the total revenue generated by the business. If all of the trade revenue is documented and properly accounted for and taxed, then there is no difference on the financial statements, balance sheets, or assets for items that were purchased with trade currency. Both cash and trade revenue are reported in the gross revenue and net revenue. The higher the revenue — the more valuable the business.

Why is this so important to understand? Because trade currency is a lot easier to earn than cash currency. If something can really help to strengthen and increase the value of your business, and it is easy to attract, why wouldn't you make this a priority item in your business practice?

If you are so busy and successful that you are turning away cash customers, then trade is probably not a good fit. If you have empty rooms, extra tables, or excess capacity where you can handle more customers, you are a perfect candidate to accept new clients with trade revenue.

In the normal business community, you need to spend money on advertising to market your business to your client base. There is no guarantee whatsoever that the money you are spending is going to result in new business. The Internet has changed a lot about how we reach new customers, but you still need to spend money in the pursuit of new customers.

The trade industry has several different components. You can call a trade broker and ask him or her to generate new business for you. Many times, you can pre-sell large blocks of a product or service in advance to get the credits you need to accomplish another task. This is not something that usually happens in the cash marketplace. If somebody is willing to pre-buy something in advance for cash, it is usually at a steep discount. In the trade industry, because everybody earns trade dollars at cost, the standard rate is the acceptable price.

You still need to plan what items you need trade dollars for. Nobody wants to be a trade millionaire. This is a taxable commodity. Proper planning will allow you to earn the amount you need in conjunction with your spending needs without increasing your tax liability.

Trade currency is an amazingly flexible product. If you have a good business, why would you limit the total potential of cash and trade revenue that your business can generate?

Chapter 9

The New Plan

As the title of this book indicates, it is time for trade to be free. With the launch of our new system, all future trade transactions within the trade system will be 100 percent free. There has been a lot of discussion about how important brokers are to the trade industry and that without a broker, members will not be able to trade on their own. I don't believe this is true. When you open a new bank account, you do not need to register to attend classes to learn how to spend money. The same is true with trade. If you know how to spend money — you already know how to spend trade.

In the barter industry, there are many layers of people who are in place to help customers with transactions. There are area directors/brokers to oversee a geographic area; there are local trade brokers/clerks to take phone calls and help transactions go through. All of these people in local offices need to get paid. It only makes sense to charge fees on all trade transactions to cover these expenses. My feeling is that these "expenses" is what is standing in the way of trade becoming a true global phenomenon and giving everybody access to a singular trade currency to make it happen.

I have stripped the model down to a single monthly fee, which covers monthly membership, maintenance of one trade account, access to online services, free monthly advertising, and mobile communication services. There are no transaction fees when you trade and there are no fees when you sell or earn credits. For a flat monthly fee, any member can trade as little or as much as they want without incurring any additional fees.

There will be differences with this new model. There will be no local offices to call. All contact will be online by computer or smartphone. All members will have access to online membership directories and be able to communicate directly with one another to complete transactions. All transactions will be posted electronically with a PIN verification system on the buyer's side of the transaction. An online marketplace will be available for members to advertise anything they want to sell to the membership. This is also a free service. There will be a customer service department that members will be able to call if they have any questions about their account, but this is not a trading desk to facilitate trade transactions. There will also be a corporate managed trade marketplace where many items will be available to the general membership.

Standard membership will be a visible membership. All standard members will be listed in the global membership directory. Only corporate members can be unlisted. To qualify as a corporate member, your company can only sell large bulk transactions directly to the corporate office. Bulk transactions will then be listed in the trade marketplace and made available to the entire membership.

There are many people within the barter industry who would strongly disagree with me about the absolute importance of brokers. Many will tell you that without brokers there would be no trade activity. Someone has to stir the pot and get the members trading, otherwise there will be little to no activity. This is one mindset.

The flip side of this argument is that brokers control the majority of trade and determine who is going to get "the good stuff" within the exchange. If capitalism has anything to say about it, then the members who pay the highest fees will see favoritism. This is a very valid complaint that many members have voiced about belonging to a barter exchange.

My personal feelings are that brokers can play an important role in certain kinds of transactions, but are not needed for the majority of transactions. I believe that the practice of a broker-centric exchange, where all members are assigned to a broker and the broker charges a percentage fee (in cash) for each and every transaction, even for the transactions where the broker is not involved, only creates walls that limit and discourage trade. I believe that the majority of members will be more than capable of utilizing free web-based tools to market their businesses and generate trade income and then search for the things they want to buy.

This creates a new opportunity where we can eliminate the single largest fee in the trade industry. By lowering the costs, many more business owners will be willing to give trade a try. The larger the trading membership grows, the greater the opportunities to trade continues to grow for all the members. The new company is being established as a member-centric organization where the overwhelming majority of members will have open access to each other and are free to negotiate whatever deals they want. By eliminating the requirement that all members must join and conduct trades through brokers, there can be no favoritism of who gets "the good stuff" and all members become equal.

So what happens to the brokers? This is where I think things will get interesting. As a former broker, I know the value that a broker can bring to the table. There will be many opportunities for transactions that can be negotiated with a trained and certified broker. The main difference will be that members will choose if and when they want to work with a broker and then both parties will need to negotiate the fee that the broker will receive to complete a certain scope of trade.

A good example would be a hotel that wants to embark on a large remodel job. There are many layers that need to be addressed for a project like this. The first being attracting enough trade currency to pay for the job. A broker can definitely assist in selling blocks of pre-paid hotel rooms. The second part involves sourcing all of the materials and craftsman to complete the list of jobs in the remodel. Many times, these large projects require large commitments from the vendors who may also require trade transactions be preset to spend the large amounts of trade all at the same time, much like tipping a line of dominoes. Party "A" gets this, party "B" gets this, and party "C" gets this.

With the new plan, the members will pay a flat monthly fee of $25, which is a monthly account maintenance fee. There is no $495 membership fee to join and there are no monthly fees in trade dollars and no cash transaction fees. That means a member can trade an unlimited amount and never incur additional fees. This removes the possibility that one member is worth more to the exchange than any other. Each member pays the same amount each month. There is no vehicle here for favoritism.

The brokers who will be working within the system are no longer acting as an all-encompassing funnel for trade and therefore cannot control who gets what. The members who want the services of a broker will be able to choose from a list of brokers as to which person will best serve their needs. Any transactions involving a broker will be negotiated between the member and the broker. The corporate office will not be a party to any broker transactions. Any fees for broker services will need to be agreed to by both the member and the broker. This is a really important feature because the new plan does not abandon the inclusion of trained professionals, it just finds a way to bring everything into balance and eliminates any obstacles to growing the world's largest trading community.

An interesting fact is that everybody likes to trade. It's fun to have people value what you have to offer and it's fun to buy goods and services from other people. Let's face it — it's fun to spend! This is the single closest comparison to cash and trade. They are both fun to spend! This positive vibe already exists in the trade industry. By eliminating the layers of cash fees, I believe we will be able to set an aggressive pace of growth and create a modern culture where trade becomes a strong secondary currency that can help any business to grow. Naturally, a lot more needs to go into creating the "secret-sauce" that will stabilize the trade currency. This is the primary responsibility of the corporate office to constantly adjust and tighten the controls to keep the global trade currency as strong as possible.

As I was developing the new plan, it dawned on me that I am really getting out of the "trade-exchange" business, because "trading" is what the members do with each other. **"Trade Coin,"** which is the name of our new venture, is moving into the "trade-currency-business." Our job is to create and manage a strong trade currency and to keep accurate records of the transactions between the members. It's exciting to see the future where one idea can grow from the past of small independent trade clubs to a global arena where the trade currency has unlimited strength and the potential to continue growing worldwide. The opportunity was always there, even in the beginning. The economics were wrong and actually limited the growth potential from being realized.

Chapter 10

How Do You Trade?

How you trade will determine the ultimate value that you will receive with your trade currency. The first thing you need to understand is that all trade credits are not equal. The trade exchange-barter industry is an unregulated financial environment. A trade exchange can open up shop anywhere it wants and can print as much trade currency as it wants.

Like all economic platforms, the results of abuse will be very easy to identify. The ideal situation would be that the sum total of trade credits in an exchange are backed by the goods and services of the members of the exchange. When the credits are tightly managed, buying power is increased because the credits have value and people want them because they know they can use them to make purchases. When you have a weak trade currency, you have an oversupply of trade credits that exceeds the amount of buying desire. In this case, you have too many credits chasing after a shrinking number of goods and services.

With a weak currency, members decline sales because they have too many trade credits that they are unable to spend. Then the problems get bigger because members need some cash in the deal to be able to accept any new trade transactions. Once you agree to start trading with 50 percent cash and 50 percent trade, the value of the trade credits will only get weaker and weaker. Ideal trade occurs when both parties agree to 100 percent trade. The reason for this is because you earn your trade dollars at your cost of goods. This allows you to realize the spread from cost to retail every time you use trade credits to make a purchase. Because you are earning at cost, you are willing to pay the full retail price when you are the buyer. In a cash deal, you would probably be more diligent in negotiating a discount and getting the best possible price for cash. With a 50/50 deal, the seller is trying to get you to pay the full retail price, because a portion is being paid with trade when in reality you would get a much better price if you paid all cash and kept your trade for a deal where your trade has more value.

If you are willing to hold the line and decline deals that do not make sense, sellers will realize that if they are not willing to trade at 100 percent — they will not get any business.

In my experience, most of the people who want some cash in the deal when they are the seller always want to be able to spend their trade credits at 100 percent when they are the buyer. This is a huge double standard that will only cause a trade exchange currency to weaken. I have thought about establishing two different levels of membership. One consisting of 100 percent traders and the other consisting of 50/50 percent traders. In the end, I do not believe that this kind of system could work. I believe that serious traders will encourage strong trade practices to prevail — if the trade currency is strong and properly managed.

So what is the solution? If the deal doesn't come together and the pricing isn't right — don't do the deal! We inherently know when we should spend our cash. If someone is charging too much, look for a better deal. With a strong online platform, it is much easier to find more options for trade. Each member of a trade exchange needs to do his part to maintain order and consistency in trading patterns. If you want to earn your trade properly, don't overcharge your prices. This is one of the culprits that gives trade a bad reputation.

The entire matter of trade management and the strength of a trade currency needs to come from the top down. The corporate structure needs to use proper restraint and maintain fiscal responsibility in infusing the right amount of trade currency into the system. Why would an exchange issue more trade credits than they need into the system? The answer is pretty straightforward. Because they need the money to cover expenses. When an exchange is small or when trading slows down, people are not spending trade credits and therefore not generating fee income. The temptation to go on a buying spree and then convert the merchandise to cash is very strong.

This is not funny, but it is something of a pattern with weak exchanges. It is kind of like a hazing ritual. New members are signed up, totally believing in the wonderful opportunities that lie ahead with their new membership in a trade exchange, and they get jumped on by a group of people who are ready to buy as much as the new members are willing to sell. Now the new members have a lot more trade credits in their account than they imagined getting. But when they try to buy something, they find out that spending their new trade is not as easy as they were led to believe.

Can this be avoided? Of course it can. The most important principle in a solid trade platform is fiscal responsibility. There are going to be losses. There are always going to be losses. Businesses go bankrupt and deals go south. These are unavoidable realities of the business world. Any serious trade exchange has to be ready to counter bad dept. It is very easy to generate bad debt by issuing too many credits. I am sure everybody believes that things will get better when new members are signed up. If you do not have an action plan to constantly renew the credit balances and erase bad debt, you are only looking at a downward spiral of debt. It starts out slowly and then the intensity increases as the debt begins to grow out of control until there is nothing left to salvage.

If you follow these steps, you should be able to count on a strong value in your trade currency:

• Accept solid deals! If the price isn't right, do not do the deal.

• Do not trust anybody with a trade transaction more than you would with a cash transaction. If someone is promising to transfer credits, but can't for whatever reason, do not deliver your goods or services until you have been paid. Trade is a relatively small community, so it is easy to trust other members. This rule applies to brokers and even employees of the trade exchange.

• Ask your trade exchange how they manage bad debt.

• Map out your trade goals. How much trade can you properly spend? How much do you need to earn to reach these goals?

• Refer new members. If you want to trade with a business that is not a member, tell them that you would gladly do business with them if they are a member of the trade exchange. If they are not willing to join, tell them that you will wait until one of their competitors joins.

• Trade with integrity.

Chapter 11

Trade As A Currency

I need to be very careful here and explain the difference between money and trade. Trade is a currency, but it is not a convertible-to-cash currency. Bitcoin is a digital crypto-currency that is redeemable to cash. Currencies like Berkshares are also purchased for cash and can be redeemed for cash. These currencies are hybrids of the monetary system.

This is the main difference between cash and trade. Trade currency was never meant to be redeemable to cash. The value of a trade currency is based on the balance of trade credits versus the goods and services of the members in a typical trade exchange system. You don't buy trade credits with cash from the company. You can buy trade credits from trade members with cash, usually at a discount, but the trade exchange company is not the seller of these trade credits. Trade is in and of itself its own currency.

Regardless of how small or large an exchange platform becomes, this practice will never change. Trade is secondary to a cash currency and stands on its own. Trade is a valuable asset and trade currency can also be traded for its own value. While the company will never redeem trade credits for cash, because that was never the intention in the creation of trade credits, this does not mean that a member of a trade exchange cannot offer to sell "their" personal trade credits to another party for cash or a cash equivalent. Trade is a valuable asset and should be treated as such.

It's funny how things change. In the old days of trade, selling your trade credits for cash at a discount was one of the big sins of trade. The trade exchanges did not like the idea of the credits being discounted, preferring that the members earn their credits by selling goods and services into the system. The members who sold credits did not want to pay 10 to 12 percent cash fees on these transactions because it ate into their spoils. Many times members have tried to figure out a way to transfer credits so as to avoid having to pay the cash service fees on the transactions. Unless the credits are in an account that you control, you do not own any credits. Getting an IOU from one member to another to avoid paying fees is about as sketchy as any transaction can be.

Under the "**Trade Coin**" plan, as there are no cash service fees, there is nothing wrong with members selling trade credits to each other whenever they want. There are many reasons why a member would be willing to sell trade credits at a discount for cash. The first reason is because they need the cash. The second reason is because there are many members who have an extremely low cost of goods and can generate a trade dollar for $0.25 to $0.35. These are primarily service-oriented businesses that do not have a hard cost of goods in their business. If your basis for the trade credits in your account is $0.25 and you can sell your credits for $0.50 to $0.75 — then you have clearly made a nice profit on the transaction.

I personally feel that too much control can detract from opportunities that would benefit the entire trade community. The value of a trade dollar is directly impacted by the desire for others to earn and hold the trade currency. If you add the new dynamic of trade currency on top of the retail business, you now add a new element that will only strengthen the overall demand for the trade currency.

As "**Trade Coin**" grows and establishes offices in foreign countries, we will introduce a global trade currency. This will be one singular currency that can be used in dozens of countries to increase trade, manufacture goods, or export services. When traveling abroad, the savings will be incredible if you can offset the costs of hotels and meals without needing to spend your cash.

When you look at the global business community, everybody wants more business. The larger our trade community grows, the larger the demand for our trade currency becomes. This is Business 101.

Chapter 12

What Can You Really Buy With Trade?

There are many different barter clubs and trade exchanges. One trade currency is not equal to another club or exchange because each has its own currency. These currencies are not interchangeable. The value is normally determined by how many "active" members belong to the organization and how stable the currency is. Did the exchange issue too much currency? Are the members all accepting new trade business? This is the real test of a trade currency. If the members are not accepting new trade business, it is because they cannot get what they want with the trade credits they already have. This is a very bad sign that things are not going well. The real value of a trade currency is completely determined by what you can buy with it.

Naturally, there will be lots of local items from service businesses and restaurants where you can buy almost anything you want at a rate that is equal to the dollar. Most businesses need at least a 50 percent or lower costs of goods to be able to trade efficiently. Car dealerships are generally not a good trading partner because the profit margins are much slimmer and the cost of goods is extremely high. You will not be able to go into the Ferrari dealer and say, "I'll take the red one!" using trade credits as payment.

This does not mean you cannot ultimately get your Ferrari with trade. Sometimes you may need to step up your trade transactions to be able to buy something you really want. You can invest in real estate or high quality art, which you can flip and sell for cash. You can offset each trade transaction by reserving the equal amount you would have spent in cash into a savings account until you reach the desired amount to go and get your car.

Trade credits can be worth more than just what you can buy from other members. The value can be much higher depending on your personal trading strategies. Many times, people need money in a hurry and are willing to sell their trade credits at a discount. A healthy trade currency will bring a higher price. While some people with a 25 to 30 percent cost of goods might feel that selling their trade credits for 50 cents on the dollar is a good deal because they are still making a profit, there are probably better deals out there.

Consider offering to pay for things for "select" people you know — who will pay you back! Let's say you offer to pay for a $500 repair bill. Rather than offering a discount, consider accepting $50 per month for 10 months without charging any interest. In 10 months you will have received all $500 back — in cash! That's 100 percent cash for your trade, which is obviously a much better deal than selling trade at a discount. You can pay for business meals or hotel stays with your trade credits and get reimbursed with cash. As trade credits are not real money, there is no platform for an investment return for holding the currency. It would make sense, then, that the best possible use of a trade currency is to keep it in motion, constantly being on the lookout for really good deals.

In the barter and trade industry, there is a lot of discussion of how you can get your full retail price when selling to other members because you are earning trade credits at your hard cost of goods. This is true for the most part; however, when someone is motivated to get a lot of trade credits, he can also be motivated to make more aggressive deals. If someone needs a lot of trade to complete another deal, he may be willing to sell something at a discounted price to keep from missing out on another opportunity.

Negotiating is part of every business transaction. It's funny how many people are willing to pay more for something when they are bidding on an online auction website. You can get all caught up in the "I want to win" attitude and find yourself bidding just to beat out other bidders. If you call a trade member and tell him that you want to buy something big but you feel the price is too high, the seller knows you have the trade credits to close the deal. If the seller is motivated to make the deal, he will call you back with a better offer. Disciplined investors are not going to pay more for something because they are caught up in the fervor. A deal should be a good deal for both parties.

Trade has value that you can leverage to ultimately get whatever you want. You just have to plot your course and make the right moves to get there.

Conclusion

I hope I have been able to give you a better understanding of how trade works. Ever since I first encountered the "modern barter" concept of trade exchanges, I have been interested in the ideology behind trading. The past 59 years has seen a lot of exchanges come and go, but I have yet to see a real economic driver come out of this industry. I believe with my new formula we will finally see true growth and multi-national expansion. This will give the professional trade environment a strong presence and the validity to establish strong relationships.

We live in difficult economic times. You can either wait for things to get better, or you can do whatever it takes to make a difference not only for you and your business, but for your community as well. I believe "**Trade Coin**" can be the leading company to grow a strong economic platform for business-to-business trade that millions of businesses can use to increase their market share and lower expenses.

I also feel that the economic platform is only one part of the total potential. It is time to pass the baton onto others to open up new markets and show us new innovations in trade that we have never seen before. Without a doubt, the larger the membership base grows, the more opportunities for amazing trade deals will develop. I hope you will consider this and give **"Trade Coin"** a spin and see what benefits are waiting for you. Let's all run a great race. See you at the finish line!

Supplemental Information

Four Things to Know About Bartering

IRS Tax Tip 2012-33, February 17, 2012 [IRS.gov]

In today's economy, small business owners sometimes save money through bartering to get products or services they need. The IRS wants to remind small business owners that the fair market value of property or services received through barter is taxable income.

Bartering is the trading of one product or service for another. Usually there is no exchange of cash. However, the fair market value of the goods and services exchanged must be reported as income by both parties.

Here are four facts on bartering:

1. **Organized barter exchanges.** A barter exchange functions primarily as the organizer of an e-marketplace where members buy and sell products and services among themselves. Whether this activity operates out of

a physical office or is internet-based, a barter exchange is generally required to issue Form 1099-B, Proceeds from Broker and Barter Exchange Transactions, annually to their clients or members and to the IRS.

2. **Barter income.** Barter dollars or trade dollars are identical to real dollars for tax reporting purposes. If you conduct any direct barter — barter for another's products or services — you must report the fair market value of the products or services you received on your tax return.

3. **Tax implications of bartering.** Income from bartering is taxable in the year it is performed. Bartering may result in liabilities for income tax, self-employment tax, employment tax, or excise tax. Your barter activities may result in ordinary business income, capital gains or capital losses, or you may have a nondeductible personal loss.

4. **How to report.** The rules for reporting barter transactions may vary depending on which form of bartering takes place. Generally, you report this type of business income on Form 1040, Schedule C Profit or Loss from Business, or other business returns such as Form 1065 for Partnerships, Form 1120 for Corporations or Form 1120-S for Small Business Corporations.

Trade Glossary

Retail Trade or Retail Barter is defined as transactions that occur between retail businesses. Businesses that participate as members of organized trade exchanges sell goods and/or services for trade credits/dollars, realizing the spread between the actual costs to provide the goods and/or services and the retail price.

Corporate Trade or Corporate Barter usually involves trade between large corporations or multi-national companies. These transactions are larger in scale than retail trade and often involve liquidating inventories and include large media buys or complex renovation projects. There are several well-established Corporate Trade companies that specialize in corporate trade transactions.

Certified Trade Broker is a trained professional who is capable of assisting members of a retail trade exchange to complete trade transactions. Services include attracting new business to earn trade credits and sourcing products and services that are needed by the member. Certified Trade Brokers usually work on a commission basis.

Trade credits are the non-cash currency of a trade exchange company. Members of a trade exchange earn trade credits by selling goods and/or services to other members of the trade exchange and are then free to spend their credits when making purchases from other members. Trade credits/dollars are not interchangeable with other trade exchanges. The actual value of a trade credit will fluctuate depending on the financial strength of the particular trade exchange. Trade exchanges with high-deficit spending will have a weaker trade currency due to too many trade credits in circulation with fewer members willing to sell, resulting in a sluggish trade economy.

Scrip is a term used by the barter industry. This word is synonymous with Gift Certificates or Gift Cards where trade credit is stored in a value certificate. Scrip certificates are usually denoted in dollar amounts and have expiration dates.

About the Author

Frank Dobrucki is a creative entrepreneur who loves designing and building new technologies. He has more than 35 years' experience in the real estate industry specializing in restructuring distressed properties, and 25 years in the trade and barter industry.

As the designer of the economic plan for "**Trade Coin**", he believes that "by making business trade available to the masses, principally by removing multiple layers of fees and eliminating control obstacles, we can finally see the modern barter age explode into a serious economic driver. It is time for all industries to embrace the positive benefit that barter brings to the table."

Frank is currently working on stackable micro-homes with the belief that many inner cities can transform decaying downtown sectors into thriving affordable centers for a young working class that is not dependent on transportation.

He is a recent graduate from Harvard University Advanced Management Development Program in Real Estate.

Business Trade Comparison

On the following page is a Business Trade Comparison chart. The top of the page previews a business without any trade sales. The numbers are straightforward and show the balance of cash sales and cash expenses to arrive at a net profit.

The bottom of the page previews the same business with the addition of 15% trade. By using the trade income to offset cash expenses, the difference is staggering! The addition of 15% trade can increase net profit by 150%.

If you feel these numbers do not make sense or that an increase of 150% is not possible, several "Worksheet" pages are included where you can input your business numbers and calculate the difference for yourself.

Try using a trade factor of 10% - 15% - 20% and see how each calculation changes with the addition of trade.

Not all businesses use trade the same way. One idea is to generate trade to only increase advertising. With pay-per-click advertising you are guaranteed a high degree of exposure because all respondents have to choose to click on your banner ad before you are charged for the click, unlike static advertising, which has no viewer controls.

You choose what you think will have the greatest impact of growing your business.

The most important thing to remember is that Numbers Do Not Lie. When you increase sales and then decrease cash spent on expenses, profits go up.

Business Trade Comparison

A Business Without Trade Sales

Cash Sales	$500,000
Trade Sales	0
Total Sales	$500,000
Cost of Goods (50%)	<250,000>
Gross Profit	$250,000

Expenses

Fixed: Wages/Taxes/Insurance/Utilities/Rent	$125,000
Variable: Advertising/Accounting/Legal/Travel Promotions	$100,000

Total Expenses
$225,000

Net Profit	$ 25,000

A Business With Trade Sales

Cash Sales	$500,000
Trade Sales (15%)	$ 75,000
Total Sales	$575,000
Cost of Goods (50%)	<287,500>
Gross Profit	$287,500

Expenses

Fixed: Wages/Taxes/Insurance/Utilities/Rent	$125,000
Variable: Advertising/Accounting/Legal/Travel Cash	$ 25,000
Promotions Trade	$ 75,000

Total Expenses		$225,000
Net Profit	**150% increase**	$ 62,500

Compare Your Business With Trade

A Business <u>Without</u> Trade Sales

Cash Sales	$_____
Trade Sales	0
Total Sales	$_____
Cost of Goods (___%)	$_____
Gross Profit	$_____

Expenses

Fixed: Wages/Taxes/Insurance/Utilities/Rent	$_____
Variable: Advertising/Accounting/Legal/Travel Promotions	$_____
Total Expenses	$_____
Net Profit	$_____

A Business <u>With</u> Trade Sales

Cash Sales	$_____
Trade Sales (___%)	$_____
Total Sales	$_____
Cost of Goods (___%)	$_____
Gross Profit	$_____

Expenses

Fixed: Wages/Taxes/Insurance/Utilities/Rent	$_____
Variable: Advertising/Accounting/Legal/Travel Cash	$_____
Promotions Trade	$_____
Total Expenses	$_____
Net Profit ___% increase	$_____

Compare Your Business With Trade

A Business <u>Without</u> Trade Sales

Cash Sales	$_____
Trade Sales	0
Total Sales	$_____
Cost of Goods (___%)	$_____
Gross Profit	$_____

Expenses

Fixed: Wages/Taxes/Insurance/Utilities/Rent	$_____
Variable: Advertising/Accounting/Legal/Travel Promotions	$_____
Total Expenses	$_____
Net Profit	$_____

A Business <u>With</u> Trade Sales

Cash Sales	$_____
Trade Sales (___%)	$_____
Total Sales	$_____
Cost of Goods (___%)	$_____
Gross Profit	$_____

Expenses

Fixed: Wages/Taxes/Insurance/Utilities/Rent	$_____
Variable: Advertising/Accounting/Legal/Travel Cash	$_____
Promotions Trade	$_____
Total Expenses	$_____
Net Profit ___% increase	$_____

Compare Your Business With Trade

A Business <u>Without</u> Trade Sales

Cash Sales	$_____
Trade Sales	0
Total Sales	$_____
Cost of Goods (___%)	$_____
Gross Profit	$_____

Expenses

Fixed: Wages/Taxes/Insurance/Utilities/Rent	$_____
Variable: Advertising/Accounting/Legal/Travel Promotions	$_____
Total Expenses	$_____
Net Profit	$_____

A Business <u>With</u> Trade Sales

Cash Sales	$_____
Trade Sales (___%)	$_____
Total Sales	$_____
Cost of Goods (___%)	$_____
Gross Profit	$_____

Expenses

Fixed: Wages/Taxes/Insurance/Utilities/Rent	$_____
Variable: Advertising/Accounting/Legal/Travel Cash	$_____
Promotions Trade	$_____
Total Expenses	$_____
Net Profit ___% **increase**	$_____

Compare Your Business With Trade

A Business <u>Without</u> Trade Sales

Cash Sales	$_____
Trade Sales	0
Total Sales	$_____
Cost of Goods (___%)	$_____
Gross Profit	$_____

Expenses

Fixed: Wages/Taxes/Insurance/Utilities/Rent	$_____
Variable: Advertising/Accounting/Legal/Travel Promotions	$_____
Total Expenses	$_____
Net Profit	$_____

A Business <u>With</u> Trade Sales

Cash Sales	$_____
Trade Sales (___%)	$_____
Total Sales	$_____
Cost of Goods (___%)	$_____
Gross Profit	$_____

Expenses

Fixed: Wages/Taxes/Insurance/Utilities/Rent	$_____
Variable: Advertising/Accounting/Legal/Travel Cash	$_____
Promotions Trade	$_____
Total Expenses	$_____
Net Profit ___% increase	$_____

Compare Your Business With Trade

A Business Without Trade Sales

Cash Sales	$_____
Trade Sales	0
Total Sales	$_____
Cost of Goods (___%)	$_____
Gross Profit	$_____

Expenses

Fixed: Wages/Taxes/Insurance/Utilities/Rent	$_____
Variable: Advertising/Accounting/Legal/Travel Promotions	$_____
Total Expenses	$_____
Net Profit	$_____

A Business With Trade Sales

Cash Sales	$_____
Trade Sales (___%)	$_____
Total Sales	$_____
Cost of Goods (___%)	$_____
Gross Profit	$_____

Expenses

Fixed: Wages/Taxes/Insurance/Utilities/Rent	$_____
Variable: Advertising/Accounting/Legal/Travel Cash	$_____
Promotions Trade	$_____
Total Expenses	$_____
Net Profit ___% increase	$_____

Compare Your Business With Trade

A Business Without Trade Sales

Cash Sales	$_____
Trade Sales	0
Total Sales	$_____
Cost of Goods (___%)	$_____
Gross Profit	$_____

Expenses

Fixed: Wages/Taxes/Insurance/Utilities/Rent	$_____
Variable: Advertising/Accounting/Legal/Travel Promotions	$_____
Total Expenses	$_____
Net Profit	$_____

A Business With Trade Sales

Cash Sales	$_____
Trade Sales (___%)	$_____
Total Sales	$_____
Cost of Goods (___%)	$_____
Gross Profit	$_____

Expenses

Fixed: Wages/Taxes/Insurance/Utilities/Rent	$_____
Variable: Advertising/Accounting/Legal/Travel Cash	$_____
Promotions Trade	$_____
Total Expenses	$_____
Net Profit ___% increase	$_____